ASTOR&NADIA

Lazaro Droznes

Published by

AVE FENIX EDITOR

ISBN-13: 978-1478335245
ISBN-10: 1478335246

ASTOR&NADIA

A big space with a large blue screen in the back.

The Boulanger space is on the right side. Two vintage armchairs on a carpet and a piano. Music sheets on the piano and on a low table. Vintage lamps light up the space. Some photos and a crucifix hanging on the wall.

On the left, the space where Astor Piazzolla lives and works in Paris. Music sheets all over like leaves in autumn. Suitcases full with music sheets. A bed covered with music sheets. A small wood desk. A lamp on the desk. Two simple chairs. On one chair a box with a bandoneón inside in black velvet.

In the proscenium on the left a small round table with two typical thonet chairs found in Paris cafes.

On the back screen different lighting can be projected to represent different weather conditions: dawn, moonlight, sunset, rain and so on.

The screen can be used also to project documentary images of Troilo, Gardel and Piazzolla, as well as images of his previous teachers like Ginastera and Rubinstein.

The orchestra, music stands and instruments are located between the two spaces and the screen.
The musicians are all dressed in black and their silhouettes can be seen against the blue screen.

The instruments are violin, double bass, guitar piano and "bandoneón".

SCENE 1
CAFÉ IN PARIS

Astor Piazzolla is a young and strong man in his mid thirties. He's seated at a typical Paris café table. A distant French song is heard. He's getting ready for a meeting. He carries a heavy suitcase and opens it carefully on the table to organize some papers. When he's finished he starts organizing all over again. He checks one page and makes some notes.

ASTOR *(directly to the public)*
Finally in Paris. I'm just about to take my first lesson with the great Nadia Boulanger. My wife and I left behind our children behind in Mar del Plata in the care of my parents and came to live the bohemian life in Paris... we're eating every other day and living in a borrowed room in a cheap hotel. But, anyhow Paris is a continous feast. I came here to make my dreams come true: leave the "bandoneón" and the tango for keeps. I'll be a composer of classical music. I have written already 20 pieces (raises the suitcase with pride). With one of these symphonies I won a fellowship to study with "la Boulanger", here in Paris. I'm in agony waiting for this "rendez vous", so expected, so decisive. I will not blow this chance. At 34 I feel like a child on the first day of school.

Astor checks his watch. Puts back all the papers in the suitcase and combs his hair with his hand. Checks again the watch, puts off the cigarette, sips the café in a hurry, leaves some coins making a gesture to a distant waiter and gets up in haste.

The light on the Paris café fades away and the light on the Boulanger space fades in.

SCENE 2
NADIA BOULANGER´S LIVING

Nadia enters the space in silence. She's an elegant mature woman aged 65 but looking 10 years younger. She's dressed with a dark suit and a fair shirt. White haired, she wears light framed eyeglasses, has brilliant eyes and serene gaze. She sits on the piano and plays Monteverdi.

Astor enters carrying the heavy suitcase. He looks around and stares at Nadia playing the piano. Suddenly, captivated by the music, he lets the suitcase fall on the floor. Nadia stops playing, turns around, gets up and goes to meet Astor in a friendly manner.

ASTOR
"Excusez-moi, Madame"

NADIA
Not Madame, please. Call me Mademoiselle, or else, just Nadia. You're Astor Piazzolla, aren't you?

ASTOR
"Oui, Mademoiselle".

Nadia makes a gesture, inviting Astor to seat. On his way Astor is distracted by a noise and begins to watch a certain spot on the floor

NADIA
Don't you worry about my cat. He's always scratching the curtains. But I won't cut his nails. It's the only thing he has to defend himself.

Nadia seats and suggests Astor do the same

NADIA
Can we talk in English? Or do you prefer French?

ASTOR
English is fine.

NADIA
All right. Monsieur Piazzolla, to be able to help you I need to know about you, not only your music. So, I'll be asking some questions. Is that all right with you?

ASTOR
It's fine with me.

NADIA
One shouldn't devote oneself to music unless you'll die if you don't do it. Are you in this predicament?

ASTOR
Absolutely Mademoiselle. My head is full of music. My life is music.

NADIA
Tell me, Monsieur. Why do you want to study?

ASTOR
At home studying was always an issue. I remember my old man yelling “you better be something big, or I’ll break your neck”

NADIA
Well, well,are you suggesting you are studying because your father commanded so?

ASTOR
Not at all. This is what I want. But, had it not been for my father I wouldn’t be here, with you, in Paris, studying music.

NADIA
At what age did you begin?

ASTOR
I discovered music at 11, in New York. It was a summer night, hot and humid. Suddenly I heard a beautiful piano. I went into shock... just listening

The pianist in the orchestra plays a Bach’s fugue that remains as background music while the conversation is on.

ASTOR
It was magic. I learned later that it was Bach, but never which piece. The musician was Bella Wilda and I started to study with him. I played classical music on different instruments. I was never a wunderkind. But... what had the most impact on me as a child was New York.

NADIA
It's interesting to discover music as a child and in New York. It's a musical city, full of noise and sound.

ASTOR
It's true. When the sirens blow together they sound like a symphony... composed by chance, different every time...

NADIA
I see you listen to music everywhere ...and you speak English very well. Were you born in New York?

ASTOR
In Argentina. But my father Nonino, emigrated to New York when I was 4. I left Mar del Plata, my friends, my grandparents, my cousins, my uncles. It was the first painful experience of my life.

NADIA
New York, as far as music is concerned, is a city that generated the roots and the fruits at the same time.

ASTOR
I carry New York very deep inside me. On the streets I learned to get tough, to take care of myself. I was raised on violent streets, with Jewish gangs, Italians, Irish... everybody against everybody. I was a friend to Jack La Motta himself, who later became a famous boxer. There, in Greenwich, I learned how to punch with the left hand. They used to call me "Lefty" (Astor mimics the left hook of a boxer)

A "knock knock" is heard on the door. Nadia gets up and receive a package full of music sheets. Nadia carries the heavy package and puts it into a drawer.

NADIA
It's from Stravinsky. He's sending his latest opus again. He does it all the time. But I don't have time to see them all. Igor is just like that, like an old man playing with his jewels. Back to you... to guide you through this journey I first have to know where is your music heading. Did you bring your work?

ASTOR
Here they are... all my sonatas and symphonies

Astor, nervous, takes the big and heavy suitcase handling it with difficulty. He begins to take out a great amount of scores and covers the little table. Nadia goes through the sheets very swiftly and stops in one. As she reads, the orchestra plays a montage of themes synchronizing with the change of sheets. It's clear Nadia can listen to the music without playing it, just from reading

NADIA
We'll listen to this one.

Nadia sits at the piano and begins to play. The light darkens to see only the scores Nadia is reading. The light fades on the orchestra beginning to play the "Sinfonietta Buenos Aires

ASTOR
It's the "Sinfonietta de Buenos Aires". With this one I won the fellowship to come to Paris. When it opened at the University of Buenos Aires auditorium, just before it started I thought "let the storm come" Imagine, to put a "bandoneón" in a symphonic concert, classical music... And so it was... A great fight broke out between those in favor and those against it. Sevitsky, who had conducted the orchestra, told me "I have never seen so many blows in an opening, but stay calm, because your music is controversial, and that's good because it means publicity"

NADIA
Don't worry about that, Monsieur Piazzolla, the same happened with Ravel's "Bolero" and Stravinsky's "Rite of Spring". You started just the same. Think of yourself as a lucky man.

ASTOR

I was accused of destroying what's sacred about classical music.

Nadia grabs the Piazzolla scores again and plays the piano. The piano from the orchestra changes the themes as Nadia goes from one sheet to the other.

ASTOR
This is the sonata I composed when ...

Nadia makes a gesture to stop Astor.

NADIA
Shhhh, please let me play and listen to your music.

ASTOR
"Excusez moi".

NADIA
Well, Monsieur Piazzolla, let's see. You compose as if you were Stravinsky. But you are not Stravinsky, music doesn't need more of the same.

ASTOR *(surprised)*
Pardon me. What did you say?

NADIA
That music doesn't need more of the same.

ASTOR
What do you mean more of the same? My music is not

more of the same!

NADIA
Don't take offense, but your music doesn't make a contribution. "C´est de la musique triviale". In those scores there is no great talent.

ASTOR
(enraged) What? Trivial? No great talent? "Excusez-moi" Mademoiselle, but I do have talent. I have talent to spare!

NADIA
Maybe. But it is not to be found here. It's music that has been done before. It has no identity.

ASTOR
Maybe you are the best teacher in the world, but you don't have the right to speak to me like that.

NADIA
All I say is for your sake. You have to trust me.

ASTOR
And you have to earn my trust.

NADIA
If you rang my doorbell and came through that door it is because you already trust me. Besides, What are you doing here? Aren't you coming precisely to develop your talent?

ASTOR
I came exactly for that, but I won't accept your denying my talent from the start! I have talent to spare. And never tell me I'm a mediocre. Ever!

NADIA
I didn't say that. I'm not saying you have no talent. I do say we don't know. Neither you nor me. Your talent, if you have any, doesn't appear in your music. Not yet. What I offer you is work, many hours of exercises, a deep and obsessive commitment to make it possible that your talent penetrates into your music, if you have any. If you don't, you'll have to accept you are just another average musician, like so many others. But without your trust there is nothing I can do.
Astor stands up, grabs the bag and heads to the door.

NADIA
I can see your temper. It's good. When you'll step onto the side walk stop and think. Don't rush, we are not in New York. You need not use your left hand here... (*Nadia makes a boxing gesture using the left hook)*

Astor in anger goes away. Nadia seats in the piano and plays Monteverdi. The piano in the orchestra starts to play
A few seconds later Astor comes back trembling, still in anger. Nada stops playing and stands up to meet him.

ASTOR
Are you challenging me?

NADIA
Exactly so, that's my job. Pushing you to discover and develop your talent, your genius. If you have it

ASTOR
I'll show you what I've got...

NADIA
You don't have to show anything. It's not necessary. What you need is to begin to work, very hard and right away

ASTOR
Very well, I accept your challenge. "Excusez moi" It's the Italian blood raised in New York. It's an explosive mix. The rage took over... I saw everything red.

NADIA
Make that rage you boast of so much work for you.... Not against you. All right... You're accepted. You can count on me from now on as your teacher, Monsieur Piazzolla. We will try very hard to uncover your genius or, if not, you'll have to accept that ... It's up to you. And now my first indication: the challenge is not with me, it's with yourself.

ASTOR
Very well, Mademoiselle.

NADIA
You must be ready for anything: to write a fugue every

week, to make three add-ons to any Haydn line, to compose an opera, some chamber music. What I deem appropriate to help you find your boundaries.

ASTOR
"D´accord, Mademoiselle"

NADIA
Fugue and counterpoint, Piazzolla, that's our business. Three times a week, from three to seven every afternoon. You will do these counterpoint exercises and fifty variations on this subject. From now on I'll be your Churchill: I have nothing to offer but blood, sweat and tears. (*impersonating Churchill voice and accent)*

Nadia stands up to finish the lesson.

Boulanger's space fades away the Piazzola's space light fades in.

SCENE 3
ASTOR PIAZZOLLA´S ROOM

Astor is doing the exercises with great effort. He writes scores. The orchestra plays fugues and counterpoints as quickly as Astor writes them. It's as if the orchestra played the music Astor has in his mind. Astor is sweating, cursing and smoking one cigarette after the other.

ASTOR *(to the public))*
God dammit, you'll see, you old Frenchy lady, who the

Gato Piazzolla is.

Astor pauses, sips a "mate" and keeps writing.

ASTOR *(to himself)*
Come on, Gato, don't give up, you can do it. Work, Commitment. Discipline. You are not an average musician.

A "bandoneòn" can be perceived in a corner, below black velvet.

SCENE 4
NADIA BOULANGER´S LIVING

Astor enters and hands Nadia a bunch of scores. As Nadia reads the sheets the orchestra plays a montage of fugues synchronized with Nadia's reading. Nadia stops in one sheet while the orchestra plays four fugues that sound slightly different but are the same.

NADIA
Astor, I asked you for four sided counterpoint and fifty variations on the same subject. Here I find 4 that look different, but they are the same. Number 4, 14, 32 y 48.

Astor starts trembling.

ASTOR *(to the public)*
Nasty old lady... she got it.

ASTOR (*To Nadia)*
But... Nadia, you hear everything

NADIA
That's right. It's easier for me to read music than to read a text. I listen to notes, always notes. I have more troubles reading the newspaper than reading a music sheet.

ASTOR
"Excusez moi,Mademoiselle". I was dead tired. You asked for 50 variations and I couldn't find the way to make them all.

NADIA
If you are a lazy student, I say "I'm not here to make your work. If you don't want to work, don't work, it's not my problem. I can only try to help you, if and when you make up your mind"

ASTOR
But my mind is totally made up. It won't happen again.

NADIA
Don't do it again, don't fool yourself. I will not accept laziness.

ASTOR
I tell myself the same thing.

NADIA

But, actually you are not as rigorous as you claim to be. That's the problem

ASTOR
It's the first time I find myself between a rock and a hard place. Now I understand that having talent is not enough to be a musician.

NADIA
So it is, Monsieur Piazzolla. Remember that to study music or any other art you need to learn the rules. But, to be able to create you have to forget them. These exercises will help you to forget the technicalities. In this fashion your voice may surface ... Can I have your works again?

Astor renders the sheets and Nadia holds them.

NADIA
Tell me. Have you ever studied seriously?

ASTOR
Yes, in Buenos Aires. Once I went to see Arturo Rubinstein when he was in town on tour. What a risk-taker I used to be! I knocked on his door. I was just 20! He opened the door and greeted me with a napkin stained with spaghetti sauce. It seems I caught hem in the middle of lunch. I told him "I'm a musician and I brought you a concert I wrote. I want you to look at it and give me your advice" Just like that.
The orchestra's pianist plays Astor's concerto.

PIANIST
"It's acceptable, but you need to study"

ASTOR
So Rubinstein recommended to start with Alberto Ginastera. I was his first student. With him I discovered Bartok, Stravinsky and their new sounds.

NADIA
Stravinsky's works are a good model for thinking and feeling. They show the subtle balance between thoughts and sentiments that needs to be achieved. Fine... Let's see what you have done, besides trying to cheat me.

Nadia holds the sheets and looks at them. As she advances the orchestra plays a montage of themes synchronized with the change of sheets.

NADIA
Let's hear this one.

Light darkens and only the music sheet Nadia is reading and the baton Astor is moving with director's strokes are seen. Light fades in on the orchestra now playing "Rapsodia Porteña"

NADIA
Please understand what I'm going to tell you. There´s no feelings here. How can I explain? I don't find Piazzolla in your works and it worries me. Where are you? It an easy question to make but very hard to answer. Many

musicians spend their lives trying to find their voice. Perfect technicians, but without feeling.

ASTOR
I feel my music nervous, poignant and aggressive. I mean to vent what happens in my life and the fury I carry inside

NADIA
It could be. But that will always be in your music. Your music can come from your heart. What is missing is to express that heart in full. We must find your style... your own and singular voice. All right. We are finished for today. See you tomorrow, Monsieur Piazzolla

ASTOR
Till tomorrow, Mademoiselle.

NADIA
Keep trying, please. Keep searching

SCENE 5.
ASTOR PIAZOLLA´S ROOM

Piazzolla is writing music sheets. The orchestra plays along. He goes wrong, starts again, lights a cigarette.

ASTOR *(to the public)*
I have to finish before Dedè returns from her painting lesson.

Astor nods to sleep. He falls asleep with the cigarette in his hand. An ash falls waking him up. Sleepy Astor puts off the cigarette and keeps sleeping seated on the chair and bent on the table.

SCENE 6
NADIA BOULANGER´S LIVING

Nadia on the piano goes through the music sheets.

NADIA
It's very well written, good technique. But... I keep asking myself: Where is Piazzolla? Piazzolla is still missing. Here you sound like Stravinsky, there like Bartok and like Ravel, but you know? I can't find you in these scores.

ASTOR
How could that be? I handle the counterpoint and fugue perfectly. But now, What shall I do? What's next? As my grandfather would say "My boat is full of fish in the middle of the storm and I have no idea where the harbor is"

NADIA
Astor, I need to know what you want. As long as I don't know what you want from music, you don't exist for me.

ASTOR
The real problem now, is that I don't exist for myself, either.

Nadia stares the bag full of music sheets. Astor follows her gaze.

NADIA

All your music lacks spirit.... Well... now we have to dive into your life. Astor, talk to me about your past. What did you do in Buenos Aires? What music did you play? Why are you so restless? Who is in fact Piazzolla? You told me you used a "bandoneón" in a symphony to cause great controversy. Why does this instrument never show up in your music again? And when you mention you played here and there you never mention the instrument. If you are hiding something, you Monsieur must tell the truth right away. We have come to a turning point. We're stagnant. If you don't speak we will not be able to move on.

Astor pauses. He gathers strength to talk stands up and walks around.

ASTOR

You are right... I'm a plain and simple "tanguero". I couldn't tell you that. Truth is I make my living making arrangements for tango orchestras. I played with Anibal Troilo, a very famous "bandoneon" player in Buenos Aires. Later on I had my own orchestra and finally, tired of it all, I began to believe my musical destiny was in classical music. And before that I made my living playing in a night-club. Until I decided to quit the tango for good

NADIA

So you are a “tanguero”. Argentine and “tanguero”. Now I understand a bit more

ASTOR
What do you understand? Tell me

NADIA
You’re a “compadrito”, one of those brave characters with real guts. In short, a tough guy! That’s exactly what is missing in your music.

ASTOR
I’m no “compadrito”! I just decided to abandon the tango, and the nostalgia that comes with it. My bandoneón...

NADIA *(interrupting)*
Certainly I want to hear it... But tell me, honestly, don’t you think that the tango also deserves a future?

ASTOR
I don’t know Madame. But, if I abandoned the tango it is because I feel it is a music focused on the past.

NADIA
Temperamental and nostalgic, we are getting to know each other. You told me that you fled from the night club, the cabaret.

ASTOR
The cabaret in Buenos Aires is a dreadful world, full of

men already dead and sad girls. I wanted my music to be more than that

NADIA
Begin by accepting that being a "tanguero" is not a mortal sin. Do we agree?

ASTOR
I didn't want to talk about it because I thought that if I told the truth, you would turn me down. Tango is popular music. You've been a school mate to Ravel, teacher of Igor Markevitch, Aarón Copland, Leonard Bernstein, Robert Casadesus, Jean Francaix, a friend to Igor Stravinsky, Paul Valery. I'm barely a tanguero. No comparison

NADIA
Tell me... How and when did you start with tango?

ASTOR
I was 8 years old when my father gave me a "bandoneon", in New York. I was expecting some roller skates and... there it was. What a disappointment! Back in Argentina I started to play with Troilo´s orchestra when I was 18.I went every evening to listen and I learned all the music sheets... by heart! One day a musician fell ill and I offered to replace him. The skeptical Troilo sits me down in the middle of the orchestra and says "So, you say you know all the music by heart? O.K kid, show me". After listening he tells me: "Kid, we play with blue suits. Tomorrow it will be with

the public"

NADIA
What you just told me is an extraordinary musical feat. Learning a repertoire by heart and being able to play it proves you are a "wunderkind". Once I heard tango on a "bandoneon" by Kurt Weill. Even Stravinsky is very fond of that instrument.

ASTOR
Don't tell me. I feel like a real...

NADIA
Don't you worry... It's all right. Well, I believe we hit the core matter. Now we are really getting to know each other. Play one of those tangos, Astor.

ASTOR
You're insinuating, Nadia, I should take all the music I've been composing for the last 10 years and throw it into the garbage can? Just like that?

NADIA
You're rushing... I didn't say that. Just play a tango, Astor, one you've composed.

ASTOR
Don't ask me to do that, Nadia. Classical music is my hope, my way to leave behind everything I hate. It's my dream.

NADIA
May be it's not a dream, maybe it's an utopia that in time may become a nightmare.

ASTOR
My nightmare is the tango.

NADIA
You think so. You don't know yet. You have the right to doubt.

ASTOR
Nadia... my bandoneón is in the closet, here in Paris, covered with mothballs and black velvet. It's been 5 years since I played it last. The only reason I brought to Paris was that if I needed money, just in case, I could always get a gig.

NADIA
Watch it. Monsieur Piazzolla, feelings that seem rock steady, may not be necessarily so. They are always renewed.

ASTOR
I have a different idea about my fate.

NADIA
I just want you to play your tango, Astor

ASTOR
Please, don't make me look backwards. My destiny is to

move on

Nadia looks at the crucifix hanging on the wall.

NADIA
Ah destiny... How can we know about destiny? Life is a miracle

Astor follows Nadia's look up to the crucifix.

ASTOR
The miracle will be making me go back to tango

NADIA
This act will not render you to the Devil. On the contrary, it may free you from your demons. Say no more, Astor. The only thing you have to do now is to play your tango. I'm listening

Astor understands he's cornered. He has no options left.

The piano in the orchestra plays "Triunfal". Astor seats and his attitude, the lightning and the "mise en SCENEe" suggest Astor is impersonated by the musician playing the "bandoneòn". Nadia listens in awe. She gets up mesmerized and moves hypnotically to the music pace drawing tango steps on the air. The music finishes and Nadia begins to come out the hypnotic state. Astor is static, waiting for Nadia's reaction. At last, Nadia puts her hand on Piazzolla`s, still on the "bandoneòn". Astor is surprised by the physical contact.

NADIA
Astor, it is my intuition that here may lie the real Piazzolla and your music. We have to move in this direction

ASTOR
You're suggesting a road I don't want to take

NADIA
You don't know where it leads. How can you be so sure?

ASTOR
That's the world I decided to quit... for good

NADIA
You can never know. Genius, if we have it, leads us. Wherever it wants us to go.

Astor raises his eyes towards Stravinsky's photo on the wall.

ASTOR
The point is that I don't care to be a popular musician. I want to get rid of the tango and the "bandoneon".

NADIA
Look... one day Ravel sent Gershwin over. He wanted to study with me. I listened for half an hour and I told him "There is nothing I can teach you"

ASTOR

You rejected Gershwin as a student?

NADIA
Gershwin had already found his voice without my help. He was composing on a regular basis, meaning that he was self disciplined already. He was already famous and didn't need social contacts. So, why would I take him up? It was a waste of time for both. There was nothing to gain and even worse: loading him with so much baggage could spoil the spontaneous quality of his melody and make him compose music like a bad Ravel. Who wants to take that risk?

ASTOR
Not with a talent like Gershwin

NADIA
Astor, I won't load you with baggage you definitely don't need to take on your journey. I will just throw away the ballast, the surplus. In painting the painter adds material where nothing was before. In sculpture the sculptor removes the surplus. My work with you is like sculpting

ASTOR
Where is my ballast?

Nadia grabs the suitcase full of music sheets Astor brought. She exaggerates its weight. Drags the suitcase towards Astor and leave it at his feet. Astor remains staring at the suitcase.

ASTOR
Please, Nadia, don't tell me that.

ASTOR *(to the public)*
What I want to do, from now on, obsessively, is music absolutely not related to tango. But I can't find my way,

ASTOR *(to Nadia)*
I vomit one million notes per second

NADIA
Stop thinking, Astor, you are competing with Beethoven or Brahms but with your demons, those who prevent you from writing your own music.

ASTOR
My demons lie in the tango

NADIA
And so do your angels. Heartless music is useless. It's no good for you neither for the world. But, on the contrary, your tango comes from the heart. You can bet on that.

ASTOR
Nadia. I'm a man with strong feelings, but I don't want to go back to tango, never again. Look, one day in Buenos Aires the orchestra played a violoncello introduction I had written for "Cups, girls and kisses"
The orchestra plays an introduction to the tango "Copas, amigas y besos"

ASTOR
The cabaret girls started to dance on tiptoes, as if it were the "Swan Lake" Imagine my rage, even the cabaret girls mocked my music.(Astor moves impersonating a classical ballet dancer)

NADIA
Astor, it's nothing to worry about.

Nadia looks and points with her hand towards the photos hanging on the wall. Astor follows.

NADIA
Bartok used to compose on the basis of Hungarian folk themes. Villa Lobos on Brazilian folklore, Manuel de Falla on Spanish music and Gershwin on jazz. You have now the unique chance of doing the same with tango. Seize the opportunity and you'll forge your destiny with your own hands. Why can't you be for Argentina what they were for their country?

ASTOR
Once Troilo was checking some arrangements I did using all I learned with Ginastera

The orchestra plays a Piazzolla´s arrangement for Troilo with some degree of innovation

MUSICIAN BANDONEONIST
Cut the bullshit, Gato. That doesn't belong in here. The people want to dance. Tango is for dancing

ASTOR
Popular taste always made me feel very restrained. People wanted orchestras to play dance music and I wanted them just to listen to my music. Popular music is not my thing. People don't like what I do. People are going in one direction, and I'm going in another one.

NADIA
Here nobody will treat you like Troilo. On the contrary. I want you to use everything you've learned and put it into your tangos. Popular music or classical music? It's like saying angel or demon. You're wrong when you think the options are classical music or tango. Dear Astor, it's classical music and tango. It is not a fusion. It is a new music. Yours. Your tango may add the fugue, the counterpoint, the Bartok pace, the atonal temptations. Perhaps this is the way to find your style: Demons and angels in a magnificent counterpoint!

ASTOR
So, going back to tango to find my style. And if it's not there? What's next?

NADIA
You're rushing again.

ASTOR
It's true; I have a satanic side and an angelical one. Satan sometimes pops up. He's there. A catcher in the rye. Ready to jump and grab me.

NADIA
A strong character is good, but you have to put it to the service of your music.

ASTOR
I still need to get rid of my memories. Those smells, miseries, sadness, green felts, caramboles, glossy leather shoes, cabaret girls, the tenements... All of that, is embodied in the tango

NADIA
A teacher can, sometimes, impose something that really belongs to him. But in your case it's you who brought it up. It is you who rejects it. What place will the tango have in your music and in your life?

ASTOR
Unfortunately, the tango is there. Always. Because I remember it or because I want to forget it. It's like those impossible loves that stay with us all our life.

NADIA
But in this case your love is possible. It's you who's causing the trouble. My job is not teaching you, even if you learn. My job is to help you to learn who Piazzolla is.

ASTOR
I am a composer of classical music.

NADIA

That is what you want to be, not what you actually are. There's a tango inside you struggling to escape. We'll free it and see where it leads us. This is, Cher Astor, your chance, the adventure you're here for: the challenge of self-discovery and self-acceptance.

ASTOR
Maybe it's my destiny, imprinted in stone, I wasn't even aware of it. In New York, when I was barely 13, I worked in the movie "The day you'll love me", with Carlos Gardel

NADIA
¡Oh la la! We know Gardel very well in France. He is the most famous Argentinean, and rather curiously, he is French. So... you're marked by fire ever since by tango

ASTOR
What happens if I discover I don't like what I am?

NADIA
It's the human condition. Nobody can flee from themselves.

ASTOR
Yesterday we went with Dedé to see Oedipus Rex. Oedipus tries desperately to find out who he is. Whatever the cost. Then he learns he killed his father and married his mother. End of story? He took out his eyes because he didn't want to see what he was

NADIA

Artists only count on themselves. You are the raw material of your own work. If you don't know who you are, there's nothing you can do. You're now Oedipus, without eyes to see yourself

ASTOR
You mean I'm blind?

NADIA
Exactly so. You are now Oedipus with no eyes. You have to make up your mind to travel the road to recover your sight.

ASTOR
When I came to Paris to study with you I imagined we would only talk about music. Never this kind of conversation!

NADIA
It's a task nobody can do but you. You are looking outside, in Stravinsky, Ravel, but the answers are only within yourself. You have to look inside, not outside.

ASTOR
Argentina is a distant country, falling off the map at the end of America. We live looking outside, towards Europe, towards Paris.

NADIA
But the answers are not here. They are there, in Argentina, in your country and, of course, inside you.

ASTOR
You talk like that because you don't know Argentina

NADIA
You`re Argentinean. Nobody can avoid his fate. You are what you are.

ASTOR
I believe in destiny. I look for it and I want it. Avoiding it is the last thing I'm willing to do.

NADIA.
Destiny is waiting. You just have to embrace it. Believe me, you're not the person you think you are...

SCENE 7.

ASTOR PIAZZOLLA´S ROOM

The light fades in on the Piazzolla space. A typical French song is heard distantly. Astor takes a box, opens it, draws the "bandoneón" grabbing the leather handles, carries it to the bed carefully and unbuttons the metal fasteners. He caresses the buttons, the ribs, the mother-of-pearl arabesques. He stretches the bellows in a long ritual to finally get a sob out from the instrument, raises the "bandoneón" up to his knees, places his hands on the buttons, closes his eyes and waits until he feels the moment has become inevitable. The first chore sounds whole, final, massive. Astor sits down and begins to write on a music sheet. The orchestra plays "Fuga y misterio".

The "mise-en-SCENEe" suggests Astor is impersonated by the "bandoneon" player in the orchestra-

SCENE 8
NADIA BOULANGER´S LIVING

Astor enters in a frenzy. Out of his mind. Carries a box

ASTOR
It was like going back to the dream girl, the impossible woman.

Astor takes the "bandoneón" out of the box and shows it with pride. He's about to play.

ASTOR
Once I played in the cabaret Gershwin's "Rhapsody in Blue"

Tha bandoneónist plays seated Gershwin's "Rhapsody in Blue"

MUSIC 1
Crazy cat!

MUSIC 2
Kid, you'll get nowhere with that, leave it for the Yankees.
Upon the last chords Astor recalls.

ASTOR

About that time I wrote a tango I like "Get ready" (Preparense). When I arrived in Paris I heard it was being played in some places. I went to get my copyright money and there it was. It's paying the rent.

Astor renders the music sheet. Nadia reads. The orchestra plays "Preparense"

ASTOR
When I came back from New York I heard something that shocked me. It struck me like a lightning bolt. It happened when I heard Vardaro and felt captivated by his perfect musical phrasing and his amazing "rubato"

The violinist stands up and plays a solo violin in "Vardaro" fashion.

NADIA
Why don't you play one of the old tangos? Here "La Cumparsita" is very popular.

ASTOR
But Nadia, you're just asking for "La Cumparsita", the tango I hate the most.

NADIA
Exactly, Monsieur Piazzolla. And we'll play it together. I listen to your "Cumparsita". Allez-y!
Astor, reluctantly, plays "La Cumparsita" on his "bandoneón", being impersonated by the "bandoneon" player in the orchestra

NADIA
Good. Now add a fugue to that melody

Astor introduces a fugue in the melody.

NADIA
And now add a counterpoint and four different variations

Astor introduces a counterpoint and three variations.

NADIA
One variation is missing, Monsieur. You've done three and I requested four.

Astor introduces a fourth variation. Then he becomes passionate and starts playing and improvising like a jazz musician

NADIA
You're doing well. I'll accompany you on the piano

Astor and Nadia plays "La Cumparsita" like two jazz musicians, improvising arrangements. They look each other, smile and go back to their instruments, passionately. The music floods the stage. The light fades to black.

SCENE 9.
NADIA BOULANGER´S LIVING

Astor enters very excited. He boasts a bundle of music sheets.

ASTOR
Mademoiselle, I don't know how the wind is blowing. I just lock myself up and I compose. I see nobody, take no strolls, no Saturdays in the Louvre, no Sundays listening to the Trinité organist. It gets dark and I don't notice it. It's dawn and I don't notice it either. Madame, I am writing one tango per day. Suddenly I know what I want and how I want it. They just come to me. One after the other. All of them different, but all of them are Piazzolla, they are all my voice

NADIA
Now you see what has to be.

ASTOR
Incredibly enough, what is more difficult are the titles. I named "Nonino" this one. I couldn't stop thinking about him. Maybe it is the longing to share all of this with my old man.

Astor tenders a music sheet. Nadia holds it and starts reading. The orchestra plays "Nonino", first tango composed in Paris.

NADIA
In Valery's words: Whoever wants to record his dreams, must be awakened.

ASTOR
I was never so awakened. It's you who woke up the sleeping Piazzolla to meet Piazzolla in Paris. Now I understand the meaning of "City of Light"

NADIA
Voici Piazzolla! I believe the tango is being born again in Paris for the whole world. The first time was when the Argentinean aristocrats brought it here in the 20`s,it was born for the world and then accepted back in Argentina. And the second time is now, again in Paris. It is my belief that, sooner or later, it will be accepted in Buenos Aires. But as a new tango.

ASTOR
That's what I want, a new tango.

NADIA
The Argentinean tango has an odd fate. It was born in Buenos Aires and raised up in Paris. Not once but twice.

ASTOR
I already feel liberated from the ashamed "tanguero" I used to be.

NADIA
Take care! They'll try to mislead you. They'll tell you that having a style is repeating oneself. Don't let them confuse you. And above all, don't betray yourself. You must reconcile what seems contradictory: do tangos as usual but with fugues, counterpoints, dissonance, a sort

of tanguero in a Stravinsky mode.

ASTOR
I don't realize where all these themes come from. When I'm finished I ask myself: Did I do it? How did they come out?

NADIA
It's the state of grace.

ASTOR
I now realize I was a resentful and pretentious "tanguero", and in top of that I believed I was an "ex-tanguero"

Astor takes a music sheet from a lean portfolio, quite different to the thick suitcase he used to carry around with the classical music sheets.

ASTOR
We recorded this tango with Lalo Schifrin, a good jazz pianist, somebody with swing. Too bad he doesn't feel the tango. But here he's all right. We named it "Bandó".
The orchestra plays "Bandó"

NADIA
Let's stay with the music. Others will come with words to explain what words can't explain.
Astor tenders another music sheet. Nadia reads. Astor looks forward, expectant.

ASTOR
You know, in Buenos Aires we don't have one way streets. In Paris they are everywhere. It's fun and to remember them I named this tango "Sens Unique"

The light fades away and Astor can be seen standing up, putting his foot on the chair and his "bandoneón" on his thigh. The light fades in on the orchestra beginning to play "Sens Unique". The bandoneonist is playing stood up.

NADIA
You stood up to play! What happened to the chair?

ASTOR
Standing up I feel the "bandoneón" better. It becomes part of my body.

NADIA
O.K., Astor, your body knows how you need to play your music. Follow it. Though, I never saw anyone standing up to play the "bandoneon"

ASTOR
We are in 1954! It's crystal clear that the tango of the nineteen hundreds is dead. We have new problems and the tango must also change.

NADIA
Your work already has the seed of the times that will come. Oddly enough the public has clear thoughts about

the past but becomes wary, skeptic, worn out or indifferent when it comes to new works

ASTOR
I feel the same.

ASTOR *(to the public)*
Where is it written that nobody can be a prophet in his own land? We have to finish this story. I'll be a prophet in my own land.

ASTOR (to Nadia)
Sooner or later they'll understand that my music is not anti-Argentine. All the contrary.

Astor pauses. The orchestra plays "Buenos Aires Hora Cero".

NADIA
And now... What's wrong?

ASTOR
Too soon I'll be returning and I don't want to. I like this country too much

NADIA
Stay a bit longer, cher Astor. You have nothing left to learn. But you are invited to our little Wednesday gatherings.

ASTOR

No, no, my children have to go back to school on April the First. I must return.

NADIA
It's necessary to balance the benefits of a family and the benefits of a life committed to art. It's the most difficult decision for an artist

ASTOR
Yesterday we went with Dedé to listen to Gerry Mulligan's Octet. It changed my mind. That's what I want to do back in Buenos Aires. Even if it looks crazy.

NADIA
The most intelligent audience is the younger one. The more available to listen to new voices.

ASTOR
In Argentina we have a thinking youth. I will win them over with the Octet.

SCENE 10.
NADIA BOULANGER´S LIVING

Astor enters swollen with pride.

ASTOR
Nadia, my dear, for the first time in my life I feel the success of my tangos. I'm known in France more than in my own country. And also in Germany.

NADIA
Yesterday I heard one of yours on the radio. "Chau Paris". A tango farewell. I was very touched.

ASTOR
Tango is perfect for farewells.

Astor hands her a music sheet. The orchestra plays "Chau Paris".

NADIA
You Astor have a jewel, a Holy Grail. It's your bandoneòn. It will take to places you never dreamt of.

ASTOR
But I do not want to make music for minorities. In time I will conquer the people. You'll see that...
Astor stops, surprised.

ASTOR
I was saying all the opposite just a few weeks ago. You, Mademoiselle, have created a new Piazzolla. I was born again, in Paris, at 34. You Mademoiselle, you embody the spirit of music.

NADIA
Living within the music world is a source of pleasure and joy which I want to share through my teachings.

ASTOR
I discovered a room full of treasures, in my own home,

that I didn't know they were there.
NADIA
Music is paradise retrieved. And it's always there, waiting, always faithful

ASTOR
I'll never forget the day you told me "Add the guitar here, take off the bandoneon there, change this" because I realized I also can make mistakes.

Nadia stares at Astor pondering her words. She makes up her mind.

NADIA
Tanguero and Argentine...

Astor opens his arms in resignation and nods.

ASTOR
I am who I am
Nadia grabs a photo and writes on it:

NADIA
Que bien tôt je vous revoie a la même place, cher Astor Piazzolla. Hope we'll soon meet in this very same place, dear Astor Piazzolla

Astor takes a photo and writes on it:

ASTOR
I will never forget my Dear Nadia Boulanger.

Astor hands her the photo and receives Nadia's. Both are moved.

NADIA
You're family now. Come whenever you want.

Astor and Nadia say goodbye with a double kiss on the cheek and an embrace.

Astor walks away from the light. The lights fade away to dark.

SCENE 11.
NADIA BOULANGER´S LIVING

The light is back in half-light. Nadia shrinks, curves and becomes a very old lady. Walking with great difficulty she seats on a wheelchair. Astor enters wearing his classical beard.

ASTOR
Do you remember me? I was your student in 1954

NADIA
How could I not remember you? You are now famous, my dear Astor. I see you have conquered what used to be your main enemy: yourself.

ASTOR
And in my country they are still discussing if what I do is tango or not. It's no longer my problem. I do Piazzolla, I

do music of Buenos Aires with the bandoneòn.

NADIA
You managed to become a prophet in your own land!

ASTOR
Not as much as I wanted. I'm more of a prophet in foreign lands than in my own

NADIA
Your music is not only popular music, now it's classical music played in concert halls all over the world. Not in cabarets. Well done! "Chapeu"!

ASTOR
Mademoiselle, without you, I wouldn't be what I am.

NADIA
We both do have the privilege that our life has been blessed by music. It conveys us outside time, makes us bigger, pushes the boundaries of our life full of sorrows, kindles the sweetness in our times of happiness and erases the trifles that cause us angst.

ASTOR
You're still listening to music in your head, all the time?

NADIA
All the time...

ASTOR

What are you listening to at this moment? Mozart? Monteverdi? Bach? Stravinsky? Ravel?

NADIA
A music that has no beginning... and has no ending.

Astor makes a musical director's gesture to the orchestra. The orchestra starts to play "Contrabajísimo"

Astor holds the Nadia's shaking hands in a goodbye gesture

ASTOR
Au revoir, Cher Mademoiselle.

NADIA
Au revoir, Cher Astor.

The orchestra keeps playing "Contrabajísimo" 30 seconds more. Astor and Nadia are frozen on stage. At last the orchestra plays the typical "chan chan" always present in the end of a tango.

THE END

REGISTRO DIRECCION NACIONAL DEL DERECHO DE AUTOR No. 425301
Buenos Aires, Argentina

Author: Lazaro Droznes
lazaro@tangovox.com

47275855R00029

Made in the USA
Middletown, DE
05 June 2019